GRAVESTONES TOMBS AND MEMORIALS

——— TREVOR YORKE ———

COUNTRYSIDE BOOKS
NEWBURY BERKSHIRE

First published 2010
© Trevor Yorke 2010
Updated and reprinted 2017

All rights reserved. No reproduction
permitted without the prior permission
of the publisher:

COUNTRYSIDE BOOKS
3 Catherine Road
Newbury, Berkshire

To view our complete range of books,
please visit us at
www.countrysidebooks.co.uk

ISBN 978 1 84674 202 6

Photographs and Illustrations by the author

Designed by Peter Davies, Nautilus Design
Produced through The Letterworks Ltd., Reading
Typeset by KT Designs, St Helens
Printed by The Holywell Press, Oxford

CONTENTS

INTRODUCTION 4

Chapter 1
CHURCHYARDS AND CEMETERIES: A BRIEF HISTORY OF BURIAL
6

Chapter 2
GRAVESTONES AND LEDGERS
16

Chapter 3
CHEST TOMBS AND MONUMENTS
28

Chapter 4
SYMBOLS AND IMAGERY
38

Chapter 5
INSCRIPTIONS AND EPITAPHS
49

FURTHER INFORMATION
59

LOCATING GRAVES, DATING GRAVESTONES, GRAVEYARDS TO VISIT
59–60

GLOSSARY
61

BIBLIOGRAPHY
62

INDEX
63

Introduction

I am as guilty as anyone of assuming that old gravestones and tombs are no more than simple records of the deceased or collectively form a backdrop to the church. I had always thought they only mustered interest when massed together in the gloriously ostentatious Victorian cemeteries. It never crossed my mind to pay too much attention to them when visiting churches whilst researching for a recent book until, while leaning upon one such memorial to steady my camera as I photographed a small Gloucestershire edifice, I became aware that I was being stared at! Stepping back in surprise I found that I had made eye contact with a skull, and standing back further realised that he was not alone. In fact the tomb I had thought of as no more than a convenient tripod was crammed with carved skeletons, figures, books and tools surrounded by lavish decoration and with a central plaque which confirmed that this work of art was nearly 300 years old.

This Eureka moment inspired me to look at my local churchyard in a new light and although I had walked through it many times before, it was only now I noticed strange carvings, mysterious symbols and humorous effigies. Here beneath a cloak of trees and ivy were fine sculpture and elegant calligraphy, centuries of changing styles which had mostly been forgotten. It was also clear that there was a lot more information about the deceased than just a name and dates. The type of stone used, the quality and quantity of carving and the additional text all gave clues to the person's standing in society.

This book sets out not only to aid the family historian or church visitor by translating some of the mysterious symbols and text, but also to open our eyes to the works of art which stand free to view. It begins by explaining the development of the churchyard and cemetery and the changes to burial practices. The second and third chapters then look at the period styles of gravestones and tombs and the shapes and features which help date them. The last two chapters look in detail at the carvings and inscriptions, showing the variety and quality which can be found and their possible meaning.

Using my own drawings and photographs I hope to inspire the reader to take a closer look at the memorials in their local graveyard, and the sculpture and tragic tales carved upon them. Some may leave with a closer connection to the deceased, an appreciation of the skill of the mason and perhaps the feeling that life is not so bad today as we sometimes feel it is!

Trevor Yorke

Introduction

FIG 0.1: *Examples of the different types of memorials and some of their details which can be found in churchyards and cemeteries.*

CHAPTER 1

Churchyards and Cemeteries
A Brief History of Burial

FIG 1.1: *An imaginary churchyard with some of the memorials and features which can be found today after over a thousand years of burial. Such has been the displacement of soil over the centuries due to reburials building up on the same spot that many churches have a trench around them and retaining walls because the ground level has risen by up to a couple of metres!*

Ivy-clad gravestones and crumbling tombs illuminated by moonlight through a gloomy ceiling of trees with only the hoot of an owl to break the eerie silence. This familiar image of the churchyard was first eulogised by poets in the 18th century, then became a vital component in the Gothic novels of the early 1800s before being crystallised in our minds by 20th-century horror films.

Yet this spooky incantation seems far removed from the neatly-trimmed landscaped sites we see today and, as you will discover, was quite different from that which preceded it. Before looking in detail at the memorials found within, it is worth explaining how churchyards have been transformed over the years, why cemeteries were founded and what features you can still find there.

The earliest forms of burial we can readily see in the landscape today are the various types of earthen mounds and stone chambers erected from the Neolithic Age up to as late as the Early Saxon period to house either a corpse or cremated remains. Archaeologists regularly uncover cemeteries which can date from the second half of the Bronze Age through the Roman period (where they were usually sited outside of town boundaries) and into the Dark Ages. One key feature they look for to help date the graves is their alignment – where they are laid out in no set direction it implies a pagan burial but

FIG 1.2: RUDSTON, YORKS: *The success of Christianity partly lay in the way the early Church adopted old pagan beliefs rather than destroying them. Many churchyards were established around existing religious sites, and some today retain a distinctive round or irregular plan which implies they were pre-Christian. Others contain ancient features like round barrows or standing stones, none more notable than this huge monolith at Rudston. Pagan symbols like this may have simply had a cross cut into them to drive out old spirits.*

> ### Christian burials
> *Christians are buried with the head at the west end of the grave facing up and the feet at the east end. It is generally said that this is so the dead will awake at the Second Coming of Christ and be able to face in the direction from which He will arrive. However, the practice of burial so the deceased can look at the rising sun predates Christianity and it is more likely to be a hangover from older religious beliefs. The bodies of most people through the Middle Ages, and the poor up until the 19th century, would have been interred in a shroud, tied above the head and feet; only the better off would usually have a coffin.*

where they are on a roughly east-west axis the deceased was probably a Christian. This can usually be tied in with when the Saxons in a region were converted by missionaries – the armies of Celtic priests and monks invading from the north and those of the Roman Church from the south during the late 6th and 7th centuries.

Although these missionaries founded churches in the newly-converted regions, very few buildings were erected, with most priests travelling out from a Minster to a designated site probably consecrated by a wooden and, later, a stone cross. The first specific mention of a churchyard is in the mid 8th century although it is likely that burials were already taking place at these revered sites, some perhaps attracted by the interment of a notable missionary or priest. By the 10th century the specific area of 'God's Acre' was being marked out by small wooden crosses in the corners. With parish churches often being founded after this period it is likely that many churchyards pre-date the building upon which they appear to centre.

Most graves throughout the Middle Ages probably had no permanent markers although temporary wooden crosses may have been inserted. The clergy and nobles were more likely to have a stone memorial: a grave slab with a cross incised down its tapering length or a short stone with a disc-shaped

FIG 1.3: *Hogsback grave markers were of Norse inspiration and can still be found in churchyards in the North as in this example from Penrith, Cumbria. Although named after their curving form they are actually meant to represent a house with the scale-shaped tiles still visible on the upper half.*

FIG 1.4: *Tall stone Saxon preaching crosses carved with symbolic figures relating biblical stories and morals to an illiterate congregation can still be found in churchyards today, mainly in the Midlands and North. Smaller types like this example may have marked a notable grave although, like most, it has lost part of its shaft so appears shorter than it originally was.*

head, which are two types that can still be found today. Burial inside for anyone but the clergy was frowned upon by the early Church and it was only from the late 13th century that it became common for the local nobility to be interred there. Their memorials usually took the form of an altar tomb, a raised chest decorated with tracery or coats of arms on later types, and an effigy of the deceased lying along the top. They would either be positioned in the chancel (the nearer to the altar the better), or in a chantry chapel, created from part of an aisle or a separate building in which mass was said for its wealthy founder. Other rich individuals who could not afford such a monument could still be buried under a stone slab or a brass, the detail retained in the

FIG 1.5: *Grave-slabs are the most common Saxon and medieval burial markers found today, with their distinctive incised crosses, and many churches have one or two propped up against a wall inside. Early ones tend to be narrow with a tapered shape and a simple cross, ones from the 13th century have a more elaborate cross carved in relief while those from the 14th century tend to be on rectangular stones. Many of these grave-slabs were lost or used in later rebuilding and often discovered during restoration. The most incredible collection was the 300 found in Bakewell church, Derbys (above), some 70 of which have been mounted in the porch where they can still be viewed today.*

FIG 1.6: *Stone coffins used for important burials, usually under the church floor, are another frequently found medieval relic. They were not, however, for permanent interment but were only used while the body decayed, the hole at the bottom allowing fluids to drain out and speed up the process. After this the bones were removed to a charnel house (either a chamber below the church, a room to the side of it or a separate building in the churchyard) after which the coffin could be used again.*

latter a useful indication of period dress and individual aspiration.

The area around the medieval church would have looked completely different from our familiar image. There would have been few if any stone memorials, the only feature standing above the hummocks of graves on the sunny south side would have been the churchyard cross mounted on a stepped base, which marked the consecrated ground. The north side would usually be bare. This shaded part was believed to be the realm of the devil and evil spirits, and even later it was used particularly for the burial of strangers, suicides and unbaptised children. In many cases it was only in the 19th century, when population growth created so much pressure for burial space, that it was put into use.

In the Middle Ages the churchyard was often the only public space in the parish, so was used for fairs, with stalls set up within the hallowed ground and sports events like archery (these would probably have taken place on the grave-free north side). The priest may also have had his house set up in a corner of the ground with his own livestock able to graze God's Acre, leading to some families planting willow or brambles to keep the animals off the graves!

The Reformation and the founding of the Church of England in the early 1530s heralded in more than a century of religious turmoil. Iconoclasts

FIG 1.7: *Although effigies were a feature of the altar tombs within the building they can occasionally be found outside in the churchyard. Those still in good condition may have been re-sited from inside, those worn so as to be unrecognisable may be in their original position. This husband and wife pair dating from around 1600 in the churchyard at Stone, Staffs were inside the medieval church but when a new building was erected a few yards away they were left stranded outside, with the gentleman losing his legs and hands during the demolition.*

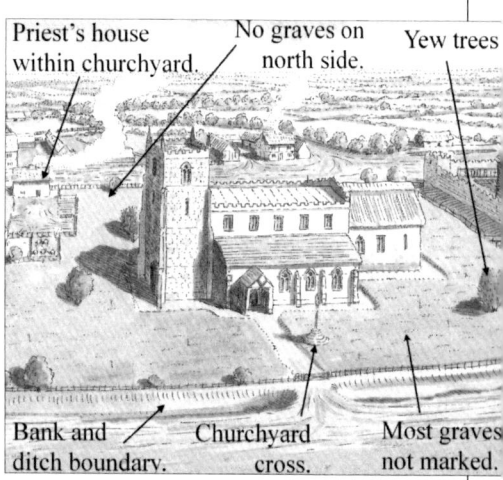

FIG 1.8: *A view over an imaginary medieval churchyard, with labels of some of the key features.*

FIG 1.9: *It is common to find the remains of the stepped base of the medieval churchyard cross on the south side of many churches today. Some remain empty while others have had a sundial mounted on them (as in this case on a short column) or a replica cross fitted.*

FIG 1.10: *We are so familiar with the grey tones of churchyard memorials that it may come as a shock to learn that many gravestones and tombs were painted sometimes with bright colours! It may have been just the sculptured upper section which had this treatment, with details and lettering picked out in gold, white or black and it probably lost its intensity within months of exposure to the elements. However, fragments on shaded parts such as splashes of red and black on this tomb in Shrewsbury can still be found today.*

destroyed any Catholic symbols, most notably the cross, and many of the memorials which did exist were lost, including the churchyard cross (the burial service was even banned under the Commonwealth, with bodies taken to the grave without ceremony or any memorial). The Restoration of the Monarchy in 1660 brought an end to many of these Puritanical extremes and coincided with a growth in the number of successful farmers, merchants and other professionals who now wanted and could afford permanent memorials in the churchyard. It is generally from the mid 17th century that the earliest gravestones and tombs will be found.

Although some Anglicans started to object to internal burials, the nobility continued to be interred inside most churches with Classical monuments, wall plaques and grave slabs filling up every available space, a practice which continued into the 19th century. Outside small markers with just the deceased's initials, decorated headstones and Classical chest tombs quickly clogged up the once open churchyard with memorials vying with each other to get as close as possible to the south side of the chancel (being buried near to the altar could be just as important outside). The effect was further enhanced by an 18th-century fashion for planting trees and erecting walls around the boundary.

Attitudes towards the dead also changed. The grave, which had largely been ignored after the burial as the deceased had moved onto a better place, was by the early 19th century seen as a link between the living family and the dead. Public displays of grief were reflected in the change to more flowery and emotional inscriptions while the grave itself was treated as the family's private property with railings and kerbs becoming fashionable.

The oft neglected churchyards crammed with headstones struggling to be seen above long grass and ivy which

FIG 1.11: *Pre-19th century gravestones generally faced away from the burial as in the top example which has a coffin stone marking the position of the grave and the text on the visible lichen-covered side. By the Victorian period gravestones had their text overlooking the deceased with the grave marked out by low railings or a stone kerb (bottom). Note though that many earlier gravestones could have been resited so may not be in their original position.*

> **Body-snatchers**
>
> The demand for fresh corpses for anatomy towards the end of the 18th century made the act of body-snatching profitable (as nobody owned the body the only crime was stealing the shroud it was wrapped in so this was usually left behind). Although the wealthy paid for heavy slabs, railings or other preventative methods to keep the body-snatchers at bay, it was the poor buried in shallow common graves which were the easiest targets. When these so-called Resurrectionists selected a single grave a narrow hole was dug down towards the head of the coffin, then the top was broken and the body dragged up by rope, thus avoiding a full excavation. The practice of body-snatching only seems to have died out after the 1832 Dissection Act which permitted the use of unclaimed bodies from hospitals and workhouses for anatomy.

Churchyards and Cemeteries

had so excited 18th-century writers were not the surroundings many Victorians sought when making weekly visits on the now more strictly observed Sabbath Day. Of greater concern, however, was the poor service from alternative private cemeteries, some of which were no more than chapels with thousands of malodorous coffins stacked up in the basements. Added to this was the public health issue with overcrowding in urban churchyards.

FIG 1.12: *Railings around graves appear from the end of the 18th century and remained popular through the 1800s. Some were possibly fitted due to the public hysteria over body-snatching but most were to mark out what was now regarded as the private family plot. Simple spearhead verticals with urns on the corners were popular early on, with more elaborate Gothic designs available in the Victorian period. Many were removed for scrap metal in the Second World War leaving behind the square lead-filled holes where they had been originally fixed.*

After decades of ignoring the problem the authorities, through a series of acts in the 1840s and 1850s, banned interments inside a church, stopped new burials in many city churchyards and opened new, landscaped public cemeteries.

These public, and the more exclusive private cemeteries quickly began to fill with memorials to all members of society, with the rich now kicked out from inside the church keen to emphasise their position in society with towering monuments, shrines and family mausoleums. The middle classes kept their heads above the masses as machine cutting and improved transport made imported marble prefabricated into statues of angels and rustic crosses affordable. The working classes (who still accounted for around 70 to 80% of the population by 1900) could now afford permanent memorials, often through burial clubs and friendly societies. Many of these memorials were small gravestones or markers with just names and dates carved upon them. The last resting place of the poorest was still usually unmarked, with some laid out in common graves (pits in which wooden coffins were stacked until full and then covered up).

Victorian legislation had also in part changed the method of burial. Graves had previously been dug to no set depth. Many were deep, especially after the Reformation, to permit further family burials on top while others were only a foot or so below the surface, which was a great problem when body-snatching was rife. Legislation passed

FIG 1.13: *Privately-funded cemeteries first appeared in the 1820s and 1830s, most notably six around London, including Kensal Green and Highgate. A series of Burial Acts between 1852–7 established the system for public cemeteries and most were laid out in wide open spaces on the then edge of the urban sprawl. Some were simply fitted into a regular-shaped urban plot (top) while others had meandering paths and carefully placed trees to make pleasant parkland (bottom). Larger ones also had sections divided off for other denominations.*

in 1847 meant that the top of the coffin had to be more than 30 inches below the surface and many local authorities, who took over responsibility for burials from the late 19th century, stipulated it should be deeper still.

The corpse itself was traditionally wrapped in a cloth shroud. Charles II had ruled it should be of wool to aid the ailing national woollen industry, a decision only overturned in the early 19th century. Where a wooden coffin could not be afforded by the poor, then a parish one may have been available to transport the corpse to the grave and it would then be reused for the next burial.

The problem of overcrowding caused by the amount of space interments take up was somewhat relieved after the eccentric Dr William Price burned his son's corpse on a Welsh hillside in 1884. The subsequent test case proved his actions were not illegal and heralded a return to cremation not used, on religious grounds, since Anglo-Saxon times.

Over the last 100 years the churchyard has again been transformed. Those which remained open to burial have often been extended with a neighbouring plot or field taken over, while those inner city ones closed by the Burial Acts were turned into gardens or lost under later building. Many have had memorials removed or stacked up against the boundary wall, in part to make mowing the grass easier. Nearly all are well tended with flowers adding a splash of colour, although it only became a common practice to place them on graves after the mid 19th century. Even Victorian cemeteries have had to adapt with memorials removed on health and safety grounds and graves even reused after barely 100 years (a surprisingly common practice). Privately-owned cemeteries had the additional problem that, when full, their income dried up and many were taken over by local authorities, who in some cases removed memorials and reused the ground for new burials. Recent listing of many monuments, tombs and gravestones has given some protection to these often disgracefully neglected works of art.

FIG 1.14: *The 'lych' gate, from the Old English word meaning 'corpse', was erected as a resting point for the coffin and its bearers as they waited to be welcomed onto consecrated ground by the vicar. Originally they would have had a stone slab or timber shelf onto which the coffin was placed, many having to be carried miles from outlying communities which didn't have a burial ground (along routes still known as corpse tracks or ways). Most of those you see today are Victorian or modern, only a few are medieval as in this example from Anstey, Herts which has a tiny room to the right side once used as the village lock-up.*

Chapter 2

Gravestones and Ledgers

FIG 2.1: *A selection of gravestones from Long Sutton, Lincs, illustrating the elaborate carving and changing styles which can be found in churchyards today. The three in the foreground show the move from the simple deep bordered type on the left with consoles on top from the early 18th century, to the Rococo style of 50 years later (centre) and the delicate Classical decoration from its final decades (right). Note also how the size increases through the century.*

Early Gravestones

Gravestones (vertical slabs as opposed to those lying flat and referred to as ledgers) come in all shapes and sizes; from small stubby grave markers to large and elaborate headstones, with a separate foot-stone marking the limit of the burial. The Romans used a version known as *stelae* and a few later Anglo-Saxon types also survive, although both are usually now inside museums or churches. Medieval gravestones were only for notable burials, principally at monastic sites and most have sunk into the ground, been built into the fabric of a church (where they can often still be seen) or were destroyed in

GRAVESTONES AND LEDGERS

FIG 2.2: *The thickness, shape and quality of inscription will vary depending upon the nature of the stone used. Prior to the 19th century it was expensive to transport masonry very far so most had to make do with that which was quarried locally. Some like the slates of the West Country and Leicestershire (left) could be sliced into thin slabs and decorated with incredibly delicate carving which has retained its sharpness today. Others, like some sandstones, were cut very thick as at Bromsgrove, Worcs (right).*

the turbulent century after the Reformation.

The earliest gravestones you are likely to find in a churchyard today date from after the Restoration of the Monarchy in 1660. These are usually simple, thick slabs only a few feet above ground level (although many

FIG 2.3: *Medieval gravestones and slabs were often used as later building material, sometimes thrown into the foundations as at Bakewell (see Fig 1.5) or fitted into external walls as here at Wharram Percy, Yorks.*

FIG 2.4: *Medieval gravestones can occasionally be found preserved inside a church. They usually are short, have a disc-shaped upper part with a cross incised (as on the right) or cut in relief (as on the left).*

FIG 2.5: *Seventeenth-century gravestones were often poorly laid out with words spread over two lines (as above, with the name Elizabeth) or have the final letters squeezed in.*

FIG 2.7: *Many early gravestones would have been no more than simple markers with the initials of the deceased. Some, like the above example, are still disc-shaped like the medieval types (Fig 2.4).*

FIG 2.6: *The seemingly sudden appearance of stone memorials outside was in part due to the mason becoming established more widely in towns and villages. His work was aided by more permanent local quarries and a client base who could afford his work. These long-forgotten artists developed their skills combining vernacular styles with those found in architectural, furniture and specialist memorial pattern books. The top example (Hereford and Worcs) has small scrolls either side of an angel's head and curtains held open, common details on late 17th- and early 18th-century gravestones.*
The bottom example shows the great regional variety which can be found, with local folk art decorating the borders (Glos).

Graveboards

In areas where there was a poor supply of stone, wooden memorials were used. A distinctive form was the graveboard, which consisted of two vertical posts with a rail or board fixed between them. They ran the length of the grave and had the information about the deceased carved along them. Although most have long since rotted away the form was replicated in stone and these can still be found, especially in southern counties.

may have sunk further), with crudely inscribed lettering which is often poorly laid out. It should be remembered that at this date there would have been few in a village who could write, possibly only the vicar or schoolmaster, and the first masons to undertake the work were probably builders rather than skilled artists. However, in just a short time, in many areas, a notably higher standard of work was being produced. These usually have a border moulded around the edge, symbols of death and time carved in the upper section and a square, arched or scrolled top. The rear of the slab might also be worked, usually with just a simple tooled pattern which was a popular treatment in the Northern counties.

Eighteenth-century Gravestones

Gravestones from the 18th century are rich and varied: some in the hands of skilled masons (their names often carved on the lowest part of the stone) are works of art, others still retain the crude and rustic charm of the previous century. One village with suitable local stone for carving, a skilled mason and clients with sufficient funds to pay for their work could have beautifully decorated gravestones, whereas only a few miles away a parish without one or all these assets could be limited to basic forms of memorial. With transport of heavy items still expensive, only a fortunate few could afford to bring in a slab from a distant county so a memorial from this period which is not in a local stone may indicate a wealthy family.

In general, gravestones grew in size through the century from around 3 ft at the beginning to up to 4 or 5 ft at the end. They also became thinner and the quality of the work generally more

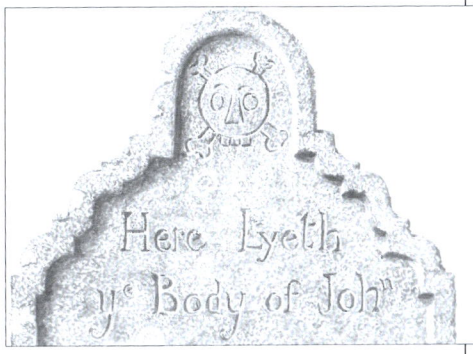

FIG 2.8: *A distinctive type of gravestone from the late 17th and early 18th centuries in Kent and Sussex had a head with a series of concave, convex and 'S'-shape pieces down each side and a semi-circular cap at the top. Some also had consoles on the sides, which look like a pair of ears.*

FIG 2.9: *A Rococo-style gravestone with labels of period features.*

refined. There was a wide selection of shapes, inspired by the Classical form of contemporary architecture and furniture design. Some had a pediment (a flat triangular feature) across the top supported on pilasters (flat columns) either side, very much like the door-

cases at the time, while others had an oval or shield surrounded by deeply-carved foliage which mirrored the Rococo style popular in the mid century. Although masons incorporated these contemporary forms into their designs, they were often mixed with local or traditional features and generally appear a decade or two after being fashionable elsewhere. Likewise, they continued long after they had fallen from favour in other forms of art, a generalisation which was still applicable into the modern age.

Gravestones in this period were still for the more affluent members of the community; mainly farmers, vicars, merchants, and professionals. Some chose plain slabs with a simple list of names and dates of the deceased for family graves with later burials added to the list. More expensive types had symbols carved around the head, many taking up the whole top third of the stone. Those from the late 17th and through to the second half of the 18th

FIG 2.10: *Many 18th-century gravestones would have been a plain slab with a square, shallow arch or profiled top and a list of family members below. For those with a little more to spend a carved upper section could be added. A short footstone repeating the initials and date of passing was also common although most have been removed or resited. (Originally it would have been on the other side of the headstone at the foot of the grave).*

FIG 2.11: *In most areas there were gravestones of unique or local style as in this example from Derbyshire!*

FIG 2.13: *The head of the finest 18th-century gravestones was usually arched or had a profile similar to contemporary chair backs and was filled with images of death (skulls) and resurrection (angels).*

FIG 2.12: *It was common for gravestones to be divided into three sections with a decorative feature in the upper third, the facts of the deceased below and an epitaph at the bottom.*

FIG 2.14: *Double-panelled gravestones for husbands and wives or family members were common up to the early 19th century. Many have a blank side, making you wonder if the other half was not as devoted as the deceased believed!*

century reflect the morbid fascination with time and death, with skulls and crossbones, hourglasses and winged cherubs' heads deeply carved in relief (the area around cut away so the pattern stands proud) or incised (the design directly cut into the stone). During the 18th and early 19th century wide slabs with two panels carved side by side (and occasionally four) intended for husbands and wives or close family members were very popular. Short footstones marking the other end of the grave were frequently used although they rarely survive today and, where they do, have often been resited up against the headstone. Body or coffin stones (see Fig 1.11) which covered the grave between these stones were also used in some parts of the country.

Early 19th-century Gravestones

In the last decades of the 18th century there was a distinctive shift in the type of symbols and decoration used on memorials. Carving became more delicate and shallow and the old morbid themes of death and time were gradually replaced by Classical imagery. Mourning female figures, weeping trees, full-length angels and urns were popular images which featured on stones; in some cases well into the Victorian period although by then they were generally confined to a smaller section at the top. In the early 19th century the Greek Revival style became influential upon gravestone design. The profile at the top was simplified with either a square, shallow

FIG 2.15: *A distinctive style popular in the first half of the 19th century was the Greek Revival. It was plain and rather austere with rectangular or tapered sides and a simple geometric profile to the top as in these, with a low triangle or pediment. Greek key decoration as in the corners of the lower example was often used.*

FIG 2.16: *Cast-iron had been used for gravestones in Kent and in the area around Ironbridge, but in the 19th century small foundries mass produced memorials from simple decorative markers with prongs to full size headstones, as in this example (they would originally have been painted).*

FIG 2.18: *Late 18th- and early 19th-century gravestones are often found with delicate carving and fine details in the Adams-style, popular a few decades earlier. In general, memorial styles are often 20 or 30 years out of date reflecting the conservative attitude of local masons away from cities like London and Bath. This example shows some of the new symbols popular in this period like the weeping tree, Hope and her anchor, and the urn.*

FIG 2.17: *Greek Revival headstones with a simple triangular head and bat wing features in the corners of the example below, and a profile replicating that of Ancient Roman and Greek* stelae *in the one above.*

triangle or arch being common forms. Decoration like swags, garlands and draped fabric remained popular and new ones with more geometric forms like Greek key were also used. Large decorated words or phrases like 'Sacred' and 'In Memory' were prominent towards the top of many stones and the inscriptions below became more emotional and sentimental.

Victorian Gravestones

The establishing of cemeteries and the rise of an affluent urban middle class in the mid 19th century coincided with great changes in the design of memorials. A reinvigorated clergy inspired by medieval Gothic architecture looked disdainfully upon what they regarded as pagan forms on Georgian gravestones and sought more appropriate styles and images, most notably with the return of the cross as a symbol (it had not been widely used since the Reformation for fear of 'Popery'). New pattern books with designs by local architects became the reference point for memorials, with Gothic arched slabs, altar tombs, coped stones and the Celtic cross prominent. However, the often uneducated middle classes preferred something more dramatic and between the ranks of elegant lancet-shaped gravestones appeared weeping angels, rustic crosses, anchors, towering obelisks and columns.

These elaborate gravemarkers became more affordable as the funeral business introduced new production techniques with prefabrication of stones and machine-cut lettering, often filled with lead inserts. Although the clergy frequently stipulated the use of local stone, cheaper imported marble from Italy, where it was sculptured near

FIG 2.19: *A selection of Victorian gravestones showing the wide variety of shapes available, although the lancet appears to be the most popular. There was often a small circular or triangular feature in the top section, containing a single weeping figure, a cross or foliage.*

The Cross
Pre-Victorian gravestones which feature the cross are rare until attitudes against Popery relaxed in the early 19th century. The Victorians made the cross popular again and the whole gravestone was shaped as thus. Plain, decorated or Celtic types are a common feature of cemeteries.

Gravestones and Ledgers

FIG 2.20: *A distinctive feature of Victorian memorials is the use of contrasting stones in a single gravestone or tomb. In this example, marble and polished granite have been inserted into the carved stone framework.*

FIG 2.21: *A Gothic-style gravestone (with a pointed arch similar to that used in 13th-century lancet windows) with labels of some features which were common on Victorian memorials.*

FIG 2.22: *Some headstones were more elaborate although not quite on the scale of the tombs and monuments of the period. The examples above are (from left to right) a broken column, obelisk, angel, and rustic cross, the latter on a pile of rocks.*

to the quarries before export, became a prominent feature in cemeteries and some churchyards. Mass production and village reorganisation as enclosure acts condensed the land into the hands of a smaller number of richer farmers, with the local gentry preferring to use their own architects to design memorials, combined to cripple the small-scale local mason and many went out of business in this period.

Ledgers, Body Stones and Coped Stones

A ledger (a flat stone laid horizontally over the grave) was a natural progression from those used during the medieval period in the floor of the church itself. They may have been preferred by those who believed they trapped the souls of the dead to prevent them coming back to haunt the living, and later it may have discouraged Resurrectionists. They can be found from all periods and in all regions but seem especially popular in the northern counties. Some are flush with the ground and tend to have grass growing over their edges, others are raised on low plinths presumably to avoid this happening, while in Cheshire and Lancashire the slabs were often used to form paths. Symbols and images are rare on ledgers except for a few simple carvings in the corners or decoration around the edge. Most are just a mass of text, recording family members, often over a number of generations, the changes in font indicating later burials beneath.

There were other stone objects used to cover the grave horizontally. The coped stone was a form of memorial used in the medieval period and into the 17th century but fell from favour until revived by the Victorians, who usually raised it upon a low plinth. It takes the form of a structure no more than a foot or so high, often with a short section at right angles to form a cross shape. Body stones were semi-circular tapering blocks laid often between the head and foot-stone, while another form was to build a coffin-shaped structure in the same position (see Fig 1.11).

All of these memorials were simple markers with text. At their finest in the 18th century they could be works of art but they pale into insignificance

FIG 2.23: *Ledgers often cover family graves and display the changing types of text over the decades and centuries as the slab was filled up.*

compared with some of the spectacular and ostentatious memorials which were built for the wealthiest members of the parish. In the next chapter we look at tombs and monuments, which have some of the finest vernacular sculpture in the country and are often just lying covered in ivy in some forgotten churchyard.

FIG 2.24: *Two types of Victorian coped stones, the left-hand example with a cross-shaped headstone, the right-hand in a cruciform plan with decorative gable ends. Note also the triangular headed gravestone with rustic log surround and the semi-circular one at the rear, two other popular forms of Victorian memorial.*

CHAPTER 3

 # Chest Tombs and Monuments

FIG 3.1: PAINSWICK, GLOS: *Rather than an upright slab at the head of a grave, a tomb was a large, usually hollow, structure of greater pretensions raised above the burial. Few graveyards have such a dramatic display as Painswick, packed with flamboyant tombs, pedestals and even a pyramid with the famous yew trees as a backdrop.*

For those in the parish with a bit more money than the middling sort – or those who wanted it to appear as such – a chest tomb might be just the sort of lasting memorial which would raise them above the ranks of ordinary gravestones. Derived from the altar tombs with which the local gentry filled their medieval churches, these were of similar proportions, roughly twice as long as wide, but without the effigy lying along the top. Although some were made from a solid block, most were hollow with the side panels slotting in or fixed with iron brackets to stone corner posts, with a large ledger placed over the top. The inside of the chest was always empty, with the body being buried below the ground in the usual manner.

The style of chest tomb changed over the years. The images and symbols used upon them follow similar lines to those on gravestones but, with the greater surface available for decoration, many tend to be more elaborate and with full-size figures. Occasionally ones from the late 16th century can be found in churchyards today, but it is more likely that the earliest you will find will date from after the Restoration. These first examples tend to have a narrow body with a thick slab across the top and a deep overhang; decoration if it is still legible is confined to heraldic panels or basic symbols, with some completely plain other than the thickly-cut lettering.

As with gravestones, the masons quickly developed their skills and before the end of the 17th century finer quality pieces were being produced. The panels became fielded (with a central section bordered by a chamfered recess like a door) and decorated with full-size figures representing time, death and resurrection on the finest examples. The corner posts could be formed into pilasters (flat columns) and the ledger reduced in bulk with a smaller overhang. This form remained popular through the 18th century and can sometimes be found in a churchyard set in a family group.

Towards the end of the century delicate and shallow-carved decoration came into fashion with the new symbols such as the urn and contemporary decoration like Greek key used on these more refined memorials. There was also a wider

FIG 3.2: *Don't be alarmed when you see a chest tomb with a cracked or missing side, a skeletal arm will not reach out to grab you! The body was always interred below ground with the hollow interior empty.*

FIG 3.3: *Early and mid 17th-century chest tombs tend to have plain thin bodies with a heavy, deep overhanging ledger on top.*

FIG 3.4: *By the late 17th century, tombs often have recessed fielded panels. Some exceptional ones have sculpture and Classical decoration; most, like the examples above, are still plain with heavy ledgers.*

FIG 3.5: *Although chest tombs are sometimes referred to as table tombs, these are more correctly a type which has no side panels but has the top ledger stone supported upon columns. They are popular in the north as in this example from Easby Abbey, Yorks.*

FIG 3.6: *Two chest tombs from the mid 18th century which now have corner posts sculptured into classical pilasters (flat columns) and less prominent ledgers on top. The top example has elaborate Rococo carving.*

Chest Tombs and Monuments

FIG 3.7: *In the late 18th and early 19th centuries there was a wide range of shapes and styles of chest tombs. Early ones had delicate carvings (bottom right), later types often were brutally simple (middle left). Sarcophagus forms (top left) and pedestals (top right) were popular as were hipped lids as on a casket (left-hand examples). Some were eclectic (middle right) with table tomb, sarcophagus and urn all in one!*

Gravestones, Tombs and Memorials

FIG 3.8: *Pedestal tombs with a smaller plan and taller body became popular from the early 19th century. This example with original railings is made from cast iron.*

range of forms available, some shaped like a sarcophagus with sloping sides narrowing towards the bottom. Others known as pedestal tombs were smaller in plan but taller, often with an urn mounted on the top.

Victorians preferred height to girth, and their tombs soared up into the sky rather than spread across the ground, a form which better suited the Gothic types of decoration. Gone was the Classical restraint of the previous period, now these spire-like memorials mounted on pedestals were encrusted with pointed arches, quatrefoils, crockets and columns, the latter often in a contrasting polished stone. Pattern books gave the Victorian monumental carver a vast array of forms and in

FIG 3.9: *A drawing of a late 18th-century (right) and a mid 19th-century tomb (left). Shallow, delicate Adams-style decoration was popular on the earlier chest tomb while pointed Gothic details dominate the vertical Victorian pedestal type.*

— CHEST TOMBS AND MONUMENTS —

FIG 3.10: *Examples of Victorian pedestal tombs with the Classical style (left) and Gothic (middle and right). Note the mix of different stones in each memorial.*

FIG 3.11: *Victorian chest tombs with pointed arched panels and flat ledgers can still be found despite the dominance of vertical memorials. In the latter decades of the century the space taken up and the ostentatious statement they made meant these tombs fell from favour and after the First World War were a rarity.*

between the ranks of lancet gravestones and obelisks in cemeteries can be found thin, wide, and occasionally completely odd tombs. The conventional chest tomb was also used, early in the period still in a Classical style, later with Gothic pointed arches down the sides.

Cotswold Tombs

There are few corners of the country where some form of elaborate tomb will not be found, but there is an unusual concentration of finely-carved and richly-sculptured types in the Cotswolds and south Gloucestershire. Many wealthy individuals had grown rich on the back of the wool trade in this area and two distinctive types of memorial were commissioned by them. In the eastern part (mainly in Oxfordshire) the Bale tomb with its

FIG 3.12: *Bale tombs with their distinctive semi-circular capping stone at Burford, Oxon. The concave ends featured scallops (above) and also cherubs and hourglasses.*

FIG 3.13: *The grooves on the bale could run side to side or diagonally, sometimes split into two opposing sections. Gadrooned bales have a large curved upper edge to the ledger with matching grooves.*

distinctive ribbed, semi-circular top was dominant. This strange form along the top of the ledger was believed to represent a bale of wool as many of the tombs were of merchants who traded in it, hence the name. It is more likely, however, to be a representation of the rippled sheet of fabric (the pall) which was draped over a semi-circular metal frame (the hearse) erected over the body during medieval funeral services (it was only from around the 17th century that the hearse became the vehicle for transporting the coffin).

In the western part and down into the Severn Vale, a different form prevailed on the finest memorials, with the ends of rectangular tombs flanked by a pair of 'S'-shaped brackets forming a distinctive lyre shape. Many of these are encrusted in all manner of contemporary sculpture and it is clear to see why they are known as Flamboyant tombs.

By the late 18th century the familiar double cube form of chest tomb was

FIG 3.14: *Flamboyant tombs in the western half of the Cotswolds had distinctive decorated ends with scrolled consols each side creating a lyre shape.*

Chest Tombs and Monuments

FIG 3.15: *One of the most sumptuously carved memorials in the country can be found in the remote graveyard at Elmore, Glos (see also Fig 4.3).*

FIG 3.16: *The scrolled consols at the edges of the end panels were probably derived from Classical decoration on the gables of Dutch-style, 17th-century houses. Between these were usually carvings of cherubs, foliage and fruit. Some also had a coat of arms, a feature which could still be found on the ends of chest tombs in the 19th century in churchyards anywhere in the country.*

FIG 3.17: *Pedestal variations of Cotswold chest tombs became popular from the late 18th century as with these examples from Painswick, Glos (often known as Tea Caddies due to their shape).*

GRAVESTONES, TOMBS AND MEMORIALS

FIG 3.18: SQUIRES MONUMENT, BURTON LAZARS, LEICS: *This elaborate and eccentric memorial, justifiably called a monument, was erected to William Squires who died in 1781. He left half of his £600 fortune for this multi-layered spectacle with a chest tomb on the lowest section and semi-circular piers at each end. Above this is a sarcophagus raised upon legs, with pie crust edging and a hollow pyramid raised on spheres on top of this. There are globes, skulls, an urn, and sculptures of Hope and Faith.*

FIG 3.19: STONE, STAFFS: *The Jervis mausoleum in a Palladian style dating from around 1760 and positioned at the popular east end of the parish church.*

a taller body on top. These pedestal tombs have more restrained decoration with stepped lids and urns on the crest and domes on the round ones; the latter were particularly popular in this region and had the nickname of Tea Caddies.

Monuments and Mausoleums

There were an exceptional few who felt they deserved something a little bit special to be remembered by. The aristocracy usually had a family chapel, filled with their memorials, in the parish church next to their country house, but increasingly from the late 17th century some built freestanding mausoleums in churchyards. After one was erected for the first time on unconsecrated ground at Castle Howard in 1726 they also began appearing within the grounds of their estates. These were classically-inspired buildings (the name coming from the ancient ruler Mausolus, whose wife

falling from fashion in the Cotswolds as it was across the country. The new form of tomb was based on a shorter rectangular, square or round plan with

Chest Tombs and Monuments

erected a huge building for him to be buried in, one of the seven wonders of the world) within which coffins of generations of aristocratic families could be stacked. They were usually designed by favourite architects or by the owner himself and have little in common with the work of funerary masons around them in the churchyard.

Those without the local standing to build such a structure on consecrated land could still stand above the tombs and gravestones around them by erecting a huge, ostentatious structure best described as a monument. These often have a chest or pedestal tomb as a starting point and then have all manner of finials, columns, obelisks and sculptures erected on top of them. In the finest Victorian cemeteries huge shrine-like structures such as these were squeezed between mausoleums and family vaults in the select corners of the landscaped burial grounds. Occasionally monuments were raised by public subscription for people more deserving of remembrance than their social superiors. Many a churchyard has a column, obelisk or unique design of memorial erected in memory of those lost in a local mining disaster or train crash, poignant reminders of the human cost of the industrial progress which bankrolled the rich laid to rest around them.

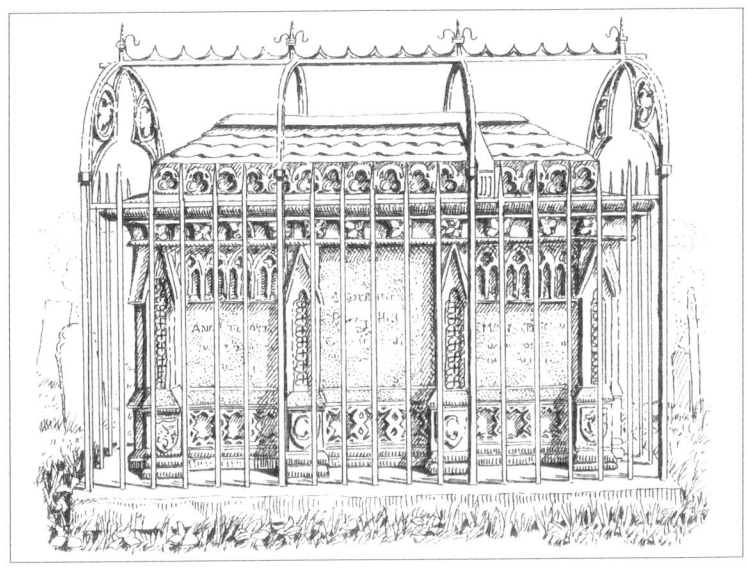

FIG 3.20: *A large Victorian tomb of the proportions of a medieval shrine encased in its original iron railings. This memorial, which is larger than a chest tomb but perhaps not quite a monument, was built in the 1850s at Sheen, Staffs, and is packed with Gothic pointed arches and trefoils with heraldic symbols along the base.*

CHAPTER 4

Symbols and Imagery

FIG 4.1: ST MARY DE CASTRO CHURCH, LEICESTER: *Many of the finest gravestones from the 17th to 19th centuries featured symbols and images in addition to the inscription. These are best preserved on slates, most notably those which can be seen in the old churches of central Leicester, carved in the north of the county.*

The most surprising aspect of many gravestones and tombs is the variety of symbolic carvings made upon them. These range from individual figures to complete scenes covering the upper half of slabs or sides of a chest. The earliest examples which can readily be seen today date from the late 17th and early 18th centuries when a fascination with mortality and time resulted in the use of symbols like skulls, crossbones, hourglasses, and the tools used to dig the grave. These became intermingled with those of a more optimistic vein, most notably angels or cherubs' heads which represent the resurrection.

Although these all can still be found

Symbols and Imagery

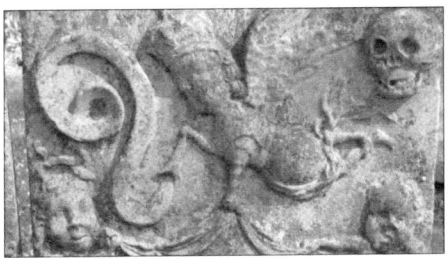

FIG 4.2: *On early gravestones the head of the stone features a number of individual symbols usually with a skull or angel's head, a grouping which represented death and resurrection, as in the top example. On the finest late 18th-century examples they tend to form a single scene, usually with a weeping figure, a tree and an urn as in the bottom left example.*

FIG 4.3: ELMORE, GLOS: *The Knowles tomb dating from the early 18th century has one of the finest displays of symbolism and sculpture. This side panel features Father Time with an hourglass and scythe on the left, standing on a wheel which represents eternity. A skeleton with sexton's tools stands upon a globe on the right, representing mortality. The central roundel has two figures in robes holding an open book while two plump angels blow trumpets behind them. At the bottom, two crouching children sit upon squashed skulls.*

in the late 18th and early 19th centuries, they have been generally replaced at this time by symbols of salvation, the figures of Hope, Faith and Charity often set under a tree, with nearly all memorials somewhere featuring an urn. By the Victorian period these dramatic scenes had fallen from favour and a compact image usually with a cross, flowers or foliage becomes common in the late 19th century.

In addition to these general carvings there were many which were favourites of individual masons. Some were just decoration copied from pattern books, architecture and furniture, or symbols from nature. Others were complete scenes composed in the head of the carver though due to their limited opportunities to travel these were probably based on somewhere in the locality. Occasionally a picture was based on an event from the Bible, while some were representations of a disaster or accident which befell the deceased.

Early symbols

FIG 4.4: ROTHLEY, LEICS: *An incredibly detailed carving of the Last Judgement with the tumbling spire based upon a neighbouring church.*

FIG 4.5: SKULLS: *These are the most simple and common symbol of death, the mortality to which we must all succumb. Some early examples are simply stylised (top) while others were more accurate (middle). They can also be found with crossbones (see Fig 4.7), scythes, sexton's tools, and in some cases with bat wings (bottom).*

Symbols and Imagery

FIG 4.7: BONES: *Two thigh bones, usually crossed, with or without a skull, form another mortality symbol. The skull and crossbones are believed to be the parts of the body required for resurrection and date back to at least the medieval period. Sometimes whole skeletons were carved but are rare, presumably because of the expensive amount of delicate carving (Fig 4.26).*

FIG 4.6: ANGELS: *These represent resurrection, the soul of the deceased on its way to heaven. There is a wide selection of local types and stylised early examples (top) while a chubby-cheeked cherub's head with wings is the most common form in the 18th century (centre top), often with Heaven represented by sun rays through clouds (centre bottom). From the early 19th century, angels are usually shown as full figures (bottom and Fig 4.13).*

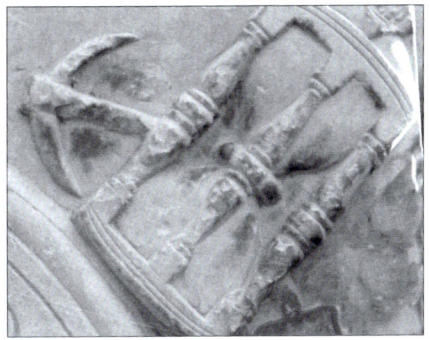

FIG 4.8: HOURGLASS: *Another popular symbol of mortality, representing the passage of time. Sometimes they were winged (bird wing means day, bat wing night). Early ones could be simplified to inverted triangles or double hearts.*

FIG 4.9: TOOLS AND TORCHES: Spades and pickaxes, the tools used by the sexton to dig graves, could mean mortality or that this was the trade of the deceased (coffins were sometimes included as well). The flaming torch shown here pointing down also signified death, but when upright meant life.

FIG 4.11: GLOBE: *Usually shown as a simple ball (sometimes with a band around the middle) it represented the pleasures of the world. It is often found offered by Death to the deceased or under a standing figure as in the above example.*

FIG 4.10: SERPENT: *The encircled serpent biting its tail means eternity. It is often wrapped around another symbol like an hourglass which linked time and eternity, or a poppy which meant eternal sleep.*

FIG 4.12: HEART: *This usually represents the virtue of Love or Charity. When shown with flames it means the fire of Divine love. It is often found pierced with a dart, although in this example it appears to be a sword (which usually represents courage or martyrdom). The three virtues mentioned by St Paul are Faith, Hope and Charity and the figures representing these were popular from the late 18th century (see Figs 4.24 and 4.25).*

SYMBOLS AND IMAGERY

4.13: TRUMPET: *This means victory and resurrection, and can be found either in the hands of angels as above or combined with mortality emblems.*

FIG 4.14: CROWN: *Symbolic of victory, honour and glory, but also can be the immortal crown of the Christian life. It is usually shown in association with other symbols, sometimes in clouds offered to the mortal below. If held in the hand, it means an innocent life, as found on the grave of a child.*

FIG 4.15: FATHER TIME: *Usually shown as an old muscular man with a scythe and hourglass, it is another symbol of time and mortality. He is depicted as a full-sized winged figure and can vary greatly, as in the two examples above.*

FIG 4.16: BOOKS: *These can represent the Bible, indicating resurrection through scripture or a member of the clergy. They can also mean wisdom and when stacked, knowledge, and can be found open or closed.*

Gravestones, Tombs and Memorials

Later symbols

FIG 4.17: DOVE: *The Divine spirit in a glory of light was a central feature of many gravestones from the last quarter of the 18th century. A dove could also mean innocence or purity and with a twig in its mouth it could mean hope or promise.*

FIG 4.18: URNS: *These generally represent the soul and when draped or leant upon by a mourning figure they form a Classical image of grief or mourning (Fig 4.23). They become common on gravestones from the late 18th century and can initially be found in delicate and varied forms (some incorrectly shown open as if they carried the human remains within) while later examples from the 1840s and 1850s are more bulky. They can be a simple central carving or a sculptured feature on top of a tomb.*

Trade Symbols

It was common for tools or symbols of trades to be included on gravestones. Carvings of crops were common on memorials to yeoman farmers and it was traditional to send a sheaf of corn to relatives upon their death. The tools of particular trades like weaving can often be found and objects like chalices or pastoral staves were used on the gravestones of the clergy. Weapons for knights and soldiers and even ships for naval officers or merchants can be found too. There are also some more peculiar trades, like the ammonites featured on the gravestone of Samuel Carrington, a 19th-century archaeologist and barrow digger!

Symbols and Imagery

FIG 4.19: TREES AND PLANTS: *A tree shown upright meant life, while one which has been cut meant death (a broken column was used in a similar way). Although a number of different types of tree can be illustrated the willow became dominant from the late 18th century through into the Victorian period. A cut flower similarly implied a life cut down in its prime, a poppy represented sleep and palm leaves or branches victory over death. Plants were regarded by many as a Popish symbol and didn't become common until the 19th century.*

FIG 4.21: LAMB: *The lamb with cross and sometimes a banner is known as the Agnus Dei, which is Latin for Lamb of God and was a popular motif on Victorian gravestones, representing Christ. It can also be found on earlier memorials set amidst flames denoting the sacrificial lamb or sometimes is associated with children's or shepherds' graves.*

FIG 4.20: HANDS: *Clasped means friendship or brotherly love while a single hand pointing could signify the Divine presence. Four hands clasped crossways was a Victorian motif inspired by a line from Tennyson: 'O for the touch of a vanished hand'.*

FIG 4.22: FREEMASONS' SYMBOLS: *A mason's gravestone showing some of the common symbols used on their memorials, although rarely in such a splendid display as this.*

FIG 4.23: WEEPERS: *Mourning figures can be found from all periods. Those holding a skull are believed to represent children who died before the parent whose memorial it is. In the late 18th and early 19th centuries a female figure weeping upon an urn or looking at a book is common (if her foot rests upon a globe it means she despised worldly pleasures).*

FIG 4.24: HOPE AND ANCHOR: *The three key virtues mentioned by St Paul were Faith, Hope and Charity (or Love) and these become popular images from the late 18th century. The figure of Hope with her anchor is very common and could be simplified to just an anchor on a pile of rock in the Victorian period.*

FIG 4.25: FAITH AND THE CROSS: *Fear of Popery meant that the cross, the primary symbol of salvation, was rarely used before the Victorian period, when it becomes common. However, if you look closely, it does appear on a number of 18th- and early 19th-century gravestones, some for Catholic families buried in more remote churchyards. Others form part of a scene along with other Passion emblems (items related to Christ's suffering on the cross) as on this example with the chalice, spear and three drops of blood falling from the clouds.*

Symbols and Imagery

FIG 4.26: DEATH SCENE: *On some more elaborate gravestones and tombs a complete death scene was carved with the deceased being pierced by a dart held by a skeleton representing Death. On other examples this gruesome character stands to one side of a central plaque, as above.*

FIG 4.27: BIBLICAL SCENES: *On some more ambitious gravestones a scene from the Bible was carved, especially in the late 18th century. The ones chosen were very much a personal choice and many have a local pastoral theme to the carving. The above example shows the Sacrifice of Isaac when God commanded Abraham to offer his son as a burnt offering but an angel, seen top right in the clouds, stopped him at the last moment.*

FIG 4.28: DISASTERS: *Occasionally a disaster like a shipwreck can be illustrated upon the gravestone. In this rare example from Great Yarmouth a suspension bridge is shown collapsing. This happened in 1845 when a clown travelling along the River Bure in a wash tub to promote a circus encouraged a crowd to surge onto the bridge causing the iron chains to break. Over 80 people, mainly children died, and the only memorial to the tragedy is this carving on the gravestone of nine-year-old George Beloe.*

Gravestones, Tombs and Memorials

FIG 4.29: ACCIDENTS: *Individual incidents can also be recorded as on this one of a pair marking the death in a train boiler explosion – a common occurrence on early locomotives – of Joseph Rutherford. Carvings like this can be historically interesting as it shows a contemporary engine. Note also this stone is painted (the current brown scheme is peeling off) as originally were other memorials (see Fig 1.10).*

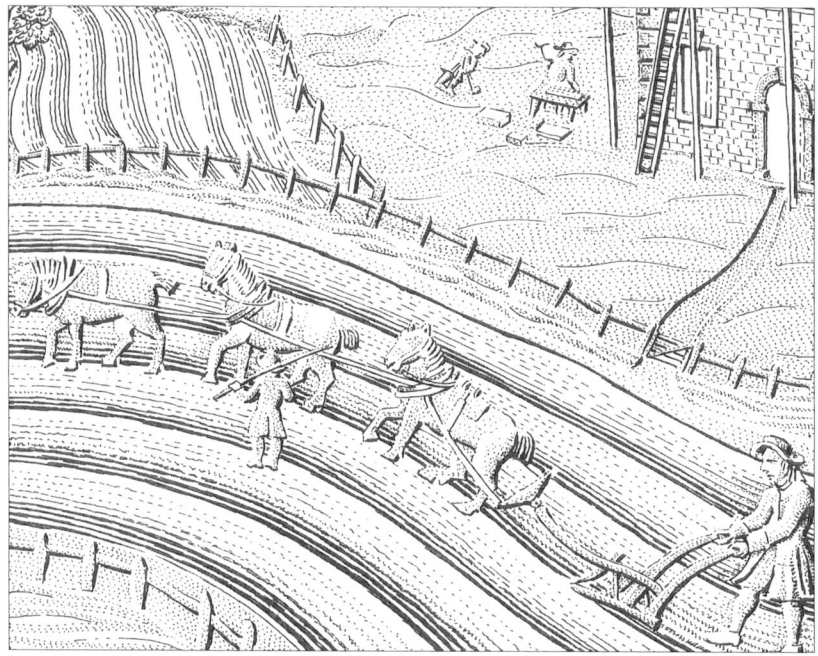

FIG 4.30: *One of the panels from the side of Sir Joseph Danver's tomb in the churchyard at Swithland, Leics, where the notable quarry produced slate for local memorials. This incredible piece shows a contemporary farming scene with ridge and furrows, ploughing and a presumably new farmhouse being built in the background. It is said that the reason this tomb is rather oddly positioned straddling the churchyard wall is that the squire wanted to be buried with his dog which could not be done on consecrated land, hence one part is outside and the other containing him is inside!*

Chapter 5

Inscriptions and Epitaphs

FIG 5.1: *The inscriptions upon gravestones vary not just in the facts they contain about the deceased but also in the style of text. Over the centuries they have ranged from simple deep cut Roman fonts (on the right) to Victorian Gothic styles (right of centre at the rear). A wide range like this can be seen in many churchyards today, the above examples all coming from Leek, Staffs.*

Locked up in the text upon gravestones and tombs is more than just the name and date of passing of the incumbent. Information can be found like the deceased's ambitions, names of relatives and attitude towards life. There may also be details like profession or cause of death and age, indicating what social conditions and life expectancy were like in the region at that time. Some gravestones were used by generations of the same family, simply listing the deceased and the date of passing, others had a single memorial typically in the 18th and early 19th century with the details of death in the centre and a poetic epitaph below. These short pieces of prose often contain further information, especially with regard to the nature of death and expectation of the afterlife. Perhaps the most striking realisation though to be gained from reading inscriptions is the fragility of life in past centuries, with records of outbreaks of disease, suffering with no pain relief, and a shockingly high infant mortality rate present in most graveyards.

Styles of Text

The style of text which was inscribed or occasionally carved in relief changed over the centuries. In the 17th century the type widely used was the Roman, crudely and deeply cut. Lettering was often poorly laid out with words split over two lines, squashed up with vertical parts combined, the occasional 'ye' added above like an after-thought and horizontal guidelines left visible. This probably reflects the fact that much of this early carving was done by

FIG 5.2: *Most gravestones are laid out as above with the introductory words at the top (the 'In' is often highlighted as with this example) and the name and details of the deceased in the middle. If you could afford the extra, an epitaph was inserted below this and in the bottom right corner (occasionally elsewhere) of some is the name of the mason or company who carved the stone.*

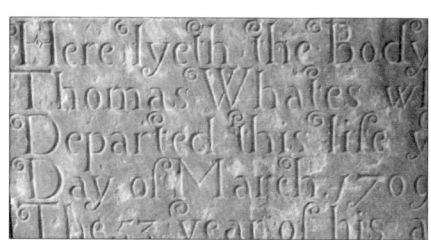

FIG 5.3: *Examples of text from 17th-century gravestones. 'Here lyeth the body' in the top example was a common opening phrase popular in this period.*

INSCRIPTIONS AND EPITAPHS

people new to the trade or as a part-time job, perhaps by a schoolmaster or vicar (often the only literate person in a village).

Standards quickly improved, however, and by the early 18th century not only was fine-quality carving to be found but also a wider range of styles. This came about due to generally increased trade and rapidly growing businesses which demanded more individual fonts for their trade cards, styles which inspired masons to imitate sometimes elaborate and flowing displays of text. These calligraphic forms were, like the decoration below, often shallow cut.

By the early 19th century the range of styles increased further with different ones often mixed on the same stone. The text was less flamboyant and calligraphic and became more formal, square and deeply cut and hence is today more legible. Fonts like San Serif, Egyptian, Grotesque and Fat Face were some of those introduced at this time while shadowing of letters was a distinctive

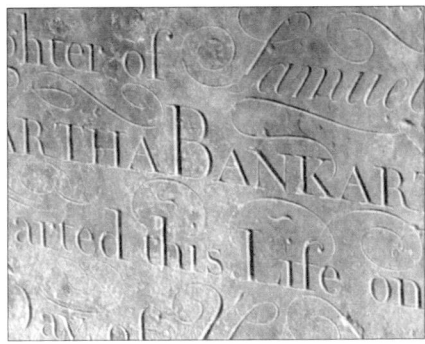

FIG 5.5: *A wide range of styles of text were available to the 18th-century mason, usually finer, shallower and more refined than those from before.*

FIG 5.4: *Eighteenth-century stones sometimes had fantastic displays of spiralling swirls and delicate calligraphy usually highlighting 'Here' or 'In' at the top.*

FIG 5.6: *Gravestones from the first half of the 19th century often have an eclectic mix of styles of text appearing like an advert for the ranges available!*

FIG 5.7: *Shadowing of text (making it appear three-dimensional) was popular in the early 19th century.*

FIG 5.9: *The Arts and Crafts movement in the late 19th and early 20th century inspired new hand-carved styles as in this example.*

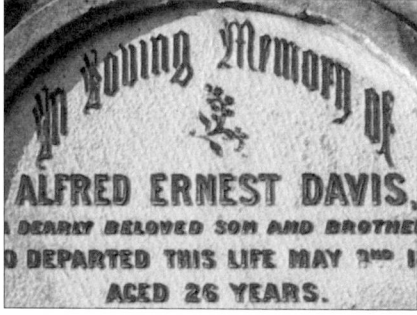

FIG 5.8: *Gothic-style text was popular on Victorian gravestones as in the larger lettering above (the top example using lead inserts). 'In sacred memory' or 'In loving memory' were popular opening lines.*

addition popular in the first half of the century.

In the Victorian period machine-cut lettering predominates and from the 1850s this was often filled with lead inserts. Gothic styles were added to those more formal types but although text is more legible it can also be uninspired and repetitive. It was only from the end of the 19th century under the influence of the Arts and Crafts movement that examples of hand-carved and more individual styles can once again be found. In the last century, despite attempts from church authorities to control the standards and materials used for gravestones, polished marble with gilt or black lettering is widespread. Yet between these the occasional individual stone can be found with hand-carved lettering inspired by calligraphy rather than the limitations of machine cutting.

INSCRIPTIONS AND EPITAPHS

FIG 5.10: *Although most gravestones in the past 100 years tend to use plain machine-cut text there are occasional memorials where a mason has hand-carved something more inventive, as in John Betjeman's gravestone shown above.*

FIG 5.11: *A very common epitaph which appears in the late 17th century and continued in use with variations into the 18th is the following: 'As you are now so once was I, As I am now so you must be'. Note when reading them that what appears to be the letter 'f' without the horizontal cross is an 's'.*

Inscriptions and Epitaphs

The earliest gravestones and tombs from the 17th century tend to have little in the way of carved inscriptions, reflecting the limited skills of those who probably did the work in their spare time. Some are simply initials and a date, others more involved but usually containing little more than names, places and dates. In the second half of the century as the trade became more professional so stones can be found with full inscriptions and a short epitaph below this. Many of these were composed by the local priest and have a distinct moral tone, yet surprisingly it is rare to find any quotes from the Bible at this date.

Eighteenth-century inscriptions have a matter-of-fact attitude towards death, often recording details of the suffering endured by the deceased. Phrases like 'a pale consumption gave the final blow' record the widespread loss of life to tuberculosis. The fact that there was little in the way of pain relief available until the early 19th century is shown in epitaphs like 'Afflictions sore long time I bore, all human help was vain, 'til God did please Death should me seize, and ease me of my pain'. The high infant mortality rate, especially in the first half of the century, is well documented on memorials; one common phrase being 'Received but yesterday the gift of breath, order'd tomorrow to return to Death'. Accidents were also recorded on many stones often with advice not to do the same. Loss in a shipwreck is common in coastal districts, while drowning is surprisingly widespread as few had reason to learn to swim.

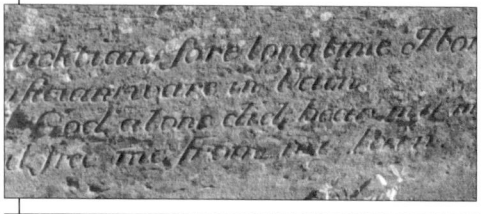

FIG 5.12: *Another common 18th-century epitaph reminds us that there was little in the way of pain relief: 'Afflictions sore long time I bore, Physicians ware in vain, Til God alone did hear my mone, And free me from my pain' (top example). Pain relief improved for the rich in the late 18th century, and became more widely available to others in the early 1800s, and 'painful death' fades away on epitaphs as a result.*

Latin inscriptions

There are a number of common Latin phrases which can be found on memorials from all periods:

Tempus erat: *Time has run out or gone.*

Memento Mori: *Means 'Remember death'.*

Sic transit gloria mundi: *This means 'So passeth away earthly glory'.*

INRI: *The initials for the Latin phrase: 'Iesus Nazarenus Rex Iudaeorum' which means 'Jesus of Nazareth, King of the Jews'.*

XP: *The first two letters of the Greek word for Christ.*

IHS: *This is used as a symbol or monogram on many 19th-century gravestones and is a contraction of the Greek word for Jesus. It could also be an abbreviation of the Latin 'Jesus, Saviour of Men'.*

There are also some English phrases which refer to life and death:

Empty tale, lighted taper, a dream, vapour, bitter draught, withering hay *or* ***a pilgrimage*** *refer to life.*

Grim reaper, assassin, wrestler, bird of prey, a frost, a tide, *and a* ***whirlwind*** *refer to death.*

Inscriptions and Epitaphs

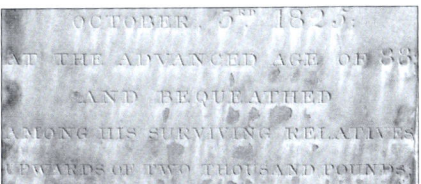

FIG 5.13: *Despite the rather grim and morbid theme to 18th-century memorial texts, there are some which record a long and healthy life. Some are clearly exaggerations or misprints with ages quoted well over 100, others are more believable as in the above example of 88. This stone also records that this gentleman bequeathed his relatives upwards of £2,000. Some 17th- and 18th-century stones also record charitable donations made by the deceased.*

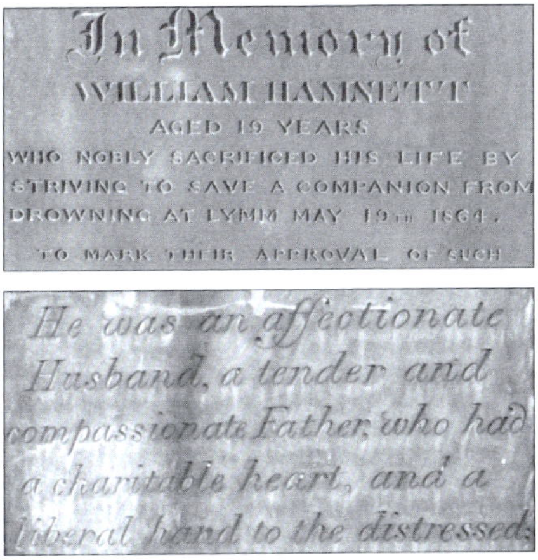

FIG 5.14: *Some inscriptions pour compliments upon the deceased, the top example because he 'nobly sacrificed his life by striving to save a companion from drowning'. The bottom example appears more of a flood of emotion typical of some from the 19th century.*

FIG 5.15: *Sudden death took away the chance for the deceased to say proper farewells or be given the last rites. The top example reads 'Farewell my Parents Brothers Sisters all, I must obey my last and greatest call; In early life while you lamenting say, Alas how sudden I was snatch'd away'. The bottom example asks the reader to reflect that 'When least expected Death may be at hand'.*

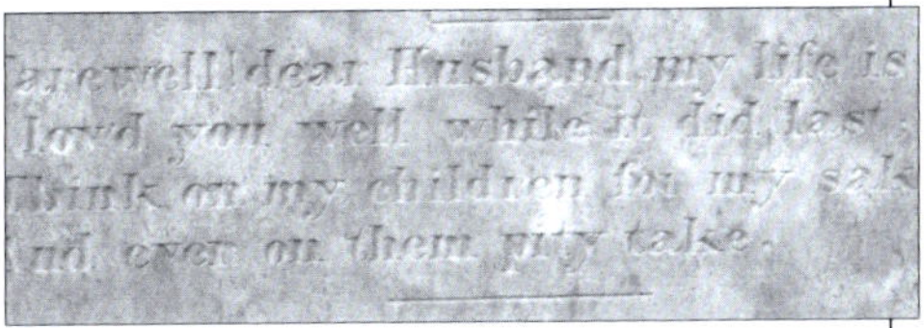

FIG 5.16: *Many 18th-century epitaphs tend to concern themselves with the family left behind, and refer to 'my wife and children dear' or 'dearest friend', with assurances that the departed is missing them and thinking about their welfare. The above example reads 'Farewell dear Husband my life is past, I loved you well while it did last, Think on my children for my sake, And ever on them pity take'.*

popular for nearly two centuries were replaced by short often repeated quotes from the Bible.

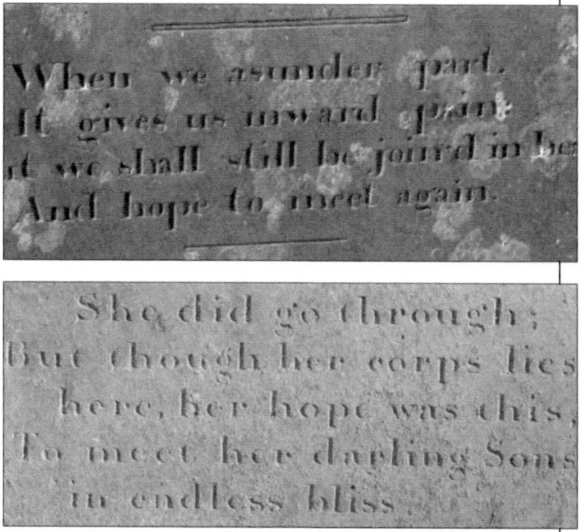

FIG 5.17: *Murder most foul is clearly the subject of this gravestone of 1786 featuring a tree with a branch broken to signify a life cut short while the hammer may be the offending weapon. The inscription below is unrestrained in its condemnation of 'a barbarous assassin', the victim describing the act as 'by murd'rous hand my thread of life was broke; Dreadful the hour, and terrible the Stroke!'*

From the turn of the 19th century the changing attitudes towards death are recorded in more romantic and sentimental epitaphs. Many use phrases like 'meet with you again' to remind them that the family would reunite in Heaven, or celebrate their passing as the resurrection of the individual with 'eternal joy' and 'rise again' widely used. Others concentrate on salvation through faith with biblical quotes becoming popular, or simple phrases like 'I have kept the Faith' or 'I have fought the good fight'. In the Victorian period the verses which had been

FIG 5.18: *The theme of resurrection and the desire of the deceased to meet their family again in Heaven are common on late 18th- and early 19th-century epitaphs. The top example states: 'When we asunder part, It gives us inward pain; But we shall still be joined in heart, And hope to meet again'. The bottom one reads: 'But though her corps lies here, her hope was this, To meet her darling Sons in endless bliss'.*

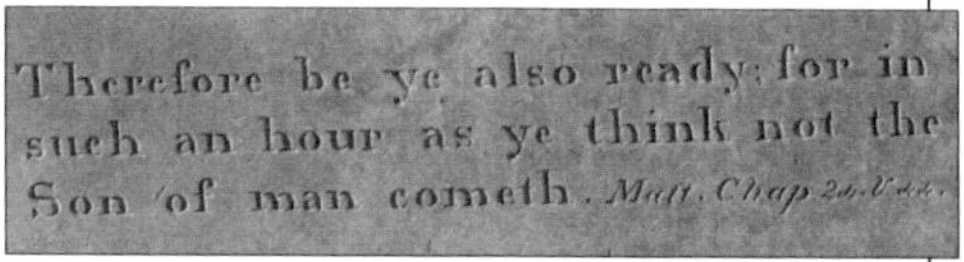

FIG 5.19: *Epitaphs tend to become shorter on Victorian memorials and were often direct quotes from the Bible as in the above example (they usually state the part of the Bible from which it is taken in smaller print afterwards).*

Inscriptions and Epitaphs

The more standardised and sentimental epitaphs used on memorials from this period often dislocate the reader from the deceased, but there is still much to be discovered about them from the facts recorded. As carved stones became more widespread for those further down the social ladder so the plight of the working classes becomes more evident, most particularly to modern eyes in the appalling infant mortality which seemed to strike many families. Large-scale natural and man-made disasters are also better recorded, in part because those most affected tended to come from a class which previously could not afford a permanent memorial. Some of the greatest losses of life due to over-ambition and cruel negligence are only recorded today in churchyards and cemeteries, to those with a keen eye.

FIG 5.20: *It seems that nearly every other Victorian gravestone records the loss of a child, all too often with their age only in weeks or months. Some have a list filling the whole stone which makes heartbreaking reading. If there is an epitaph, it tends to encourage the parents to believe that they have gone to a better place as in this example:* 'This lovely bud so young and fair, Cut of in early bloom; Just come to show how sweet a flower, In paradise could bloom'.

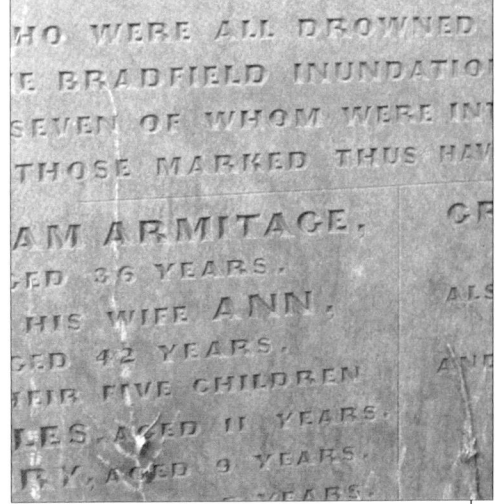

FIG 5.21: *The glories of Victorian engineering are often celebrated with plaques and statues in memory of the engineers; their failures are usually forgotten about and can only be found recorded on gravestones of those affected. On 12th March 1864 a huge dam nearing completion at High Bradfield in the hills above Sheffield burst due to a flaw in its design, sending 600 million gallons of water in a tidal wave up to ten feet high down the valley and into Sheffield. As it was at night there was little warning and over 250 people died in what is still the worst man-made disaster in this country. It is only in the churchyards and cemeteries along the route of the flood that this catastrophe is recorded. The excerpt above from the Armitage family gravestone states that the grandmother, her two sons, their wives and seven children all perished in what they term an 'inundation'. Many of the inscriptions state that some of the bodies were never found.*

FIG 5.22: *On 16th June 1883 a couple of thousand children were packed into the Victoria Hall in Sunderland to see a magic show when, towards the end, free gifts were offered so those on the gallery rushed to the stairs to get down to the stage. It is not known who jammed the door at the bottom of the stairs but as the children piled down and hit the obstruction they quickly massed up, crushing and suffocating those underneath, their weight preventing the desperate adults below from getting them out – 183 children died that day. One Sunday school of 30 lost every member while other parents turned up to find their whole family had been cruelly extinguished. Although the public memorial in the park opposite the now demolished hall has recently been restored, it is through the gravestones in the local cemetery that the loss of life is most sensitively recorded. The top left example records that the Mills lost four children and the right-hand stone the parents' anger as their children 'were killed in the dreadful calamity at the Victoria Hall'.*

FIG 5.23: *Occasionally, humour can be found amidst the mourning. This simple memorial at Eyam, Derbyshire, to the cricketer Henry Bagshaw simply has the hand of the Almighty pointing back to the pavilion as the stumps are knocked over below.*

Further Information

Locating Graves

Finding a specific grave for a family member and, hopefully, a surviving gravestone or tomb can be tricky. There was no legal requirement to record the place of burial on the death certificate, so the best source of information may be from your own family records, a receipt, copy of a will or an old Victorian memorial card. Local public records may also help, like newspaper announcements.

The most likely place where they would be buried is in the church of the parish in which they last resided (or the local cemetery) or the one which is the traditional family home. The burial registers for municipal cemeteries are held by the local authority; those for the churchyard are usually within the building itself or, for older ones, in the local records office. The precise position of the grave should be noted in cemetery records or their grave book, but churchyard records are rarely so helpful so unless a local historical society or family history group have recorded them you will simply have to start looking!

Family history websites are the most convenient place to start finding a grave. The list on page 61 contains some of the most useful which can help you find burial records. Other information and contacts can be found in the wide range of family history magazines on the market.

Dating Gravestones

The styles of text and shape of stones and tombs listed in this book can help to narrow the date range when a stone may have first been carved, if the information upon it is illegible. Where a date may be clearly carved upon a stone it should not necessarily be taken for granted that this was when the stone was first carved, especially pre-Victorian memorials. Many were bought as family stones to be used by successive generations; the first lines (usually at the top) may have eroded while later ones lower down may survive, giving the impression the stone is younger than it is. If a gravestone seems significantly earlier in form than the date upon it, then it could have been reused and occasionally the original carving is still legible on the reverse or near the base. Also, remember that although the position of a stone is a clue to the importance of the deceased, many have been subsequently resited.

The Hardy Tree, Old St Pancras Churchyard, London: A peculiar arrangement of gravestones set around an ash tree which has since spread its roots throughout them. The gravestones were set in this position when the Midland Railway were clearing part of the old churchyard in around 1865 to make way for their new St Pancras Station. The novelist Thomas Hardy had to oversee the removal of the old burials and may have been responsible for arranging the gravestones in this manner.

GRAVESTONES, TOMBS AND MEMORIALS

Places to Visit

There are thousands of graveyards around medieval churches, some of which have been used for over a millennium, creating such a displacement of soil that the level of the area is raised above the surroundings. Many will have stones and tombs of note although they may be rather lost behind monotonous later memorials. Many churchyards have had stones cleared to aid mowing, but even here some of the finest have been retained around surrounding walls.

The following is a list of a few of my personal favourites which have exceptional gravestones and memorials.

Greyfriars Kirkyard, Candlemaker Row, Edinburgh EH1 2QQ: Many impressive memorials and a couple of mortsafes which were used to protect graves from resurrectionists.

St Mary's Church, Whitby, Yorks, YO22 4DW: Memorable churchyard set high upon the cliffs next to the abbey.

St Mary's Church, Peel Ln, Astbury, Cheshire, CW12 4RG: Good collection of legers and a medieval canopied tomb.

All Saints Church, S Church St, Bakewell, Derbyshire, DE45 1FD: Exceptional collection of Saxon and Medieval grave-slabs and coffins by the porch and Saxon crosses and other stones of interest.

St Lawrence's Church, Church Street, Eyam, Hope Valley S32 5QH: A number of gravestones of plague victims from the 1660s.

St Mary's Church, Market Place, Long Sutton, Lincs, PE12 9JJ: One of the finest collections of gravestones covering all periods.

St Mary de Castro Church, Castle View, Leicester, LE1 5WN: Exceptional collection of slate gravestones from 18th and 19th century with all fine details intact. St Margaret's Church, St. Margaret's Way, LE1 3EB, also of note.

St Michael's Church, Church Street, Madeley, Shropshire, TF7 5BN: Notable for collection of cast iron gravestones and tombs.

St John's Church, Kidderminster Rd, Bromsgrove, Worcs, B61 7JW: Examples of distinctive thick sandstone gravestones and unique train boiler explosion graves.

St John the Baptist Church, Church Green, Burford, Oxon, OX18 4RY: One of the best collections of bale tombs.

St John the Baptist Church, Elmore, Gloucestershire, GL2 3SP: Notable chest tombs on south side of church (opposite entrance side) esp Knowles Tomb. Also worth visiting nearby churchyards at St Peter's Church, Haresfield, GL10 3EQ, and St Nicholas's Church, Gloucester Rd, Standish, GL10 3EU.

St Mary's Church, Long Sutton.

Places to Visit

St Mary's Church, New St, Painswick, Glos, GL6 6QB: Famous churchyard with exceptional collection of pedestal and chest tombs:

St Peter and St Paul's Church, Lavenham, Suffolk, CO10 9SA: Neatly arranged collection of late 18th and early 19th century stones.

Large Victorian cemeteries make for some of the most spectacular and interesting burial grounds. A few of note are listed here. Please be respectful when visiting and check opening times before venturing out.

Glasgow Necropolis, Castle Street, Cathedral Square, Glasgow, G4 0RH:
www.glasgownecropolis.org

Undercliffe Cemetary, Undercliffe Ln, Bradford, Yorks, BD3 0QD:
www.undercliffecemetery.co.uk

Arnos Vale Cemetery, Bath Rd, Bristol BS4 3EW: www.arnosvale.org.uk

Brookwood Cemetery, Brookwood, Surrey, GU24 0BL:
www.brookwoodcemetery.com

Highgate cemetary, Swain's Lane, London, N6 6PJ:
www.highgatecemetery.org

Abney Park Cemetery, High St, Stoke Newington, London N16 0LH:
www.abneypark.org

Kensal Green Cemetery, Harrow Rd, London W10 4RA:
www.kensalgreen.co.uk

Useful websites:
www.parishregister.co.uk.
www.deceasedonline.com
www.ancestry.co.uk
www.findmypast.co.uk
www.ffhs.org.uk
www.thegenealogist.co.uk
www.freebmd.org.uk
www.nationalarchives.gov.uk
www.ukbmd.org.uk
www.genesreunited.co.uk
www.gravestonephotos.com
www.scottishgraveyards.org.uk
www.nls.uk/family-history/gravestones (national library scotland)
www.archaeologyscotland.org.uk/our-projects/scottish-graveyards
www.gravestonestudies.org
www.york.ac.uk/spsw/research/cemetery-research-group

 # Bibliography

English churchyard memorials, Frederick Burgess, 1963 (reprinted 2004)
English churchyard memorials, Hilary Lees, 2000
Churchyards of England and Wales, Brian Bailey, 1987
Buildings of England series, Nikolaus Pevsner and others. County guides which include details on notable memorials inside and outside of churches.

Gravestones, Tombs and Memorials

Glossary

Bale tomb: A chest tomb with a grooved semi-cylindrical section along the top. Found in the eastern Cotswolds.

Body-stone: A stone shape lying horizontally between the head and foot-stone (covering the burial) and shaped like a coffin (flat, raised or semi-cylindrical).

Canopy: An ornamental stone covering above a medieval tomb.

Capital: The top decorated or grooved section of a column.

Cartouche: A panel with a curved and scrolled edging.

Cenotaph: Means an 'empty tomb' and is a monument commemorating a distant burial.

Chamfer: A diagonal cut off a square edge.

Chest tomb: A stone box built up over the burial which resembles a Classical sarcophagus or medieval altar tomb.

Console: An 'S'-shaped bracket.

Coped stone: A low memorial with a gabled top.

Discoid: A short stone marker with a round or octagonal head.

Effigy: A sculpture of the deceased lying down along the top of a medieval tomb.

Epitaph: A rhyme or comment about the deceased which is usually carved below the names and dates on memorials.

Festoons: Classical decoration of draped fabric (swags) or garlands of fruits or flowers.

Gable: Triangular shaped upper part of a wall matching the profile of the roof.

Graveboard: Horizontal plank or rail supported by two posts and running up the side of the grave, carved with details of deceased (also known as dead-board).

Hogsback: A late Saxon memorial shaped like a long house, sometimes with animals and found in Northern (Danish influenced) counties.

Ledger: A horizontal slab covering the burial with details of the deceased carved upon it (can be raised upon a short plinth).

Mausoleum: A large family tomb which can be the size of a small free-standing building.

Necropolis: Means the 'city of the dead' but is often used to refer to large Victorian cemeteries.

Obelisk: A tall stone pillar, square in plan, which tapers to a pyramid top.

Ogee: An 'S'-shaped curve or arch.

Pedestal tomb: A tall tomb with a square, round or polygonal plan, often with an urn on the top.

Pediment: A low triangular-shaped feature supported on columns projecting from the end or centre of a classical building. Used as a decorative feature on some gravestones and tombs.

Pilaster: A flat column, in this case carved into the surface of a gravestone or tomb.

Quatrefoils: A foil is a round lobe used in Gothic decoration, with the prefix 'quatre' meaning four, and 'tre' meaning three. Arranged like a clover leaf.

Rococo: A flamboyant mid 18th-century style characterised on memorials by deep foliage and convex panels.

Sarcophagus: Means 'flesh eater' and originally referred to stone coffins but now used to describe a Classical memorial in the shape of a casket or bath tub.

Stela: A Classical form of upright stone, often with a top formed from triangles.

Table tomb: A flat ledger raised upon columns in each corner so it appears as a hollow chest tomb.

Weepers: Carved figures in mourning.

Index

Altar tombs: 9, 24
Angels: 5, 13, 21, 24, 25, 38, 39
Anstey, Herts: 15
Astbury, Cheshire: 60

Bakewell, Derbys: 8, 9, 60
Bale tombs: 33–34, 60, 61
Body-snatchers: 12
Body stones: 26, 61
Bromsgrove, Worcs: 17, 48, 60
Burford, Oxon: 34, 60
Burton Lazars, Leics: 36

Cemeteries: 13, 24, 26
Charnel house: 9
Cherubs, winged: 22, 38
Chest tomb: 5, 28–36, 60, 61
Churchyard cross: 10–11
Coffins: 9, 13, 60
Coffin stone: 12
Columns, broken: 5, 24, 25
Coped stone: 5, 24, 26, 61
Cremation: 14
Crosses: 13, 24, 25, 46, 60

Elmore, Glos: 35, 60
Eyam, Derbys: 58

Flamboyant tombs: 34–35
Footstones: 5, 16, 20, 22
Freemasons: 45

Gothic revival: 24, 25
Graveboards: 5, 19, 61
Great Yarmouth, Norfolk: 47
Greek Revival: 22–24

Haresfield, Glos: 60
Headstones: 5, 16–26
Hogsbacks: 8, 61
Hourglasses: 22, 38, 41

Iron memorials: 23, 32, 60

Lavenham, Suffolk: 60
Ledgers: 5, 16, 26, 29, 30, 60, 61
Leek, Staffs: 49
Leicester: 38, 60
Long Sutton, Lincs: 16, 60
Lych gate: 15

Madeley, Salop: 60
Mausoleums: 13, 36–37, 61
Monuments: 5, 13, 36– 37

Obelisk: 5, 24, 25, 62

Painswick, Glos: 28, 35, 60
Pedestal tomb: 5, 31–36, 60, 62
Penrith, Cumbria: 8

Reformation, The: 10–11, 13, 17
Restoration, The: 11, 17, 29
Rococo: 20, 30, 62
Romans: 7–8, 16, 23
Rudston, Yorks: 7

Saxons: 7–8, 16, 60
Sheen, Staffs: 37
Sheffield, Yorks: 57
Shrewsbury, Salop: 11
Shrines: 13
Skulls: 21, 38–41
Standish, Glos: 60
Stone, Staffs: 10, 36
Sunderland, Tyne and Wear: 58
Swithland, Leics: 17, 48

Table tombs: 30, 62
Trees: 22, 23, 39, 45

Urns: 22, 23, 32, 39, 44

Weepers: 39, 46, 62
Wharram Percy, Yorks: 17

OTHER TITLES FROM COUNTRYSIDE BOOKS

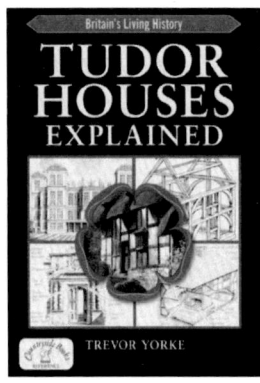
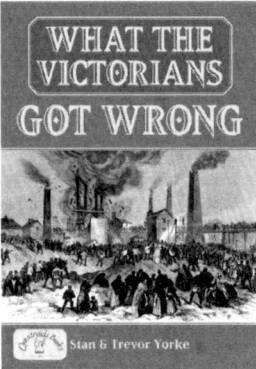
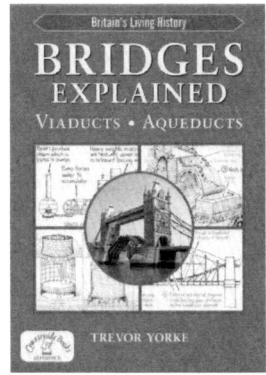

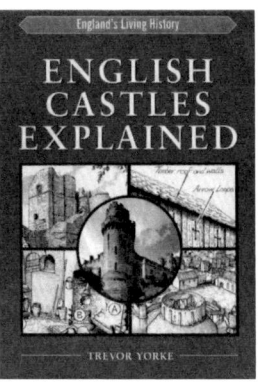
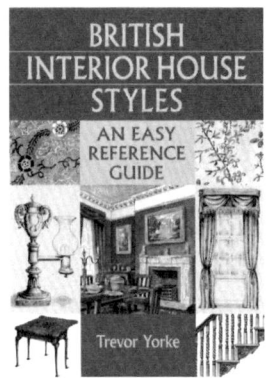

To see the full range of Trevor's books please visit
www.countrysidebooks.co.uk or **www.trevoryorke.co.uk**

Follow us on  @CountrysideBooks